Alonzo E. (pseudonym) Dramond

Dramond

A Secret Of The Midway Plaisance

Alonzo E. (pseudonym) Dramond

Dramond

A Secret Of The Midway Plaisance

ISBN/EAN: 9783741197352

Manufactured in Europe, USA, Canada, Australia, Japa

Cover: Foto ©Andreas Hilbeck / pixelio.de

Manufactured and distributed by brebook publishing software (www.brebook.com)

Alonzo E. (pseudonym) Dramond

Dramond

Secret

OF THE

Midway Plaisance

By ALONZO E. DRAMOND.

Press of Byron S. Adams,
Washington, D. C.

Secret of the Midway Plaisance.

REWARD, $50,000.

JENNINGS & COMPTON, ATTORNEYS AT LAW,
TRAFALGAR SQUARE,
LONDON, ENGLAND.

The above reward will be promptly paid to any one giving information leading to the finding of a young boy by the name of Tyler Edgar Wilson, who suddenly disappeared from London on the first day of June, 187—. The following is a detailed description of young Wilson: Age, eight years; height, about four feet, nine inches; color of eyes, dark blue; complexion, fair. Master Wilson when last seen wore a light suit of cheviot, a white shirt with ruffled front, patent leather shoes. He also had with him a small gold watch upon which his name was engraved and on the inner side was his mother's picture.

For further particulars, appply to
JENNINGS & COMPTON,
Attorneys at Law,
Trafalgar Square,
London, England.

The above startling notice appeared some years ago the London papers, and the entire English Capital is immediately aroused. Every one knew the

Wilsons, their ancestral line could be traced back to time immemorial; their mansion was one of the most elegant in all London and was noted for the hospitality and generosity of its owner.

Mr. Elbert Wilson, whose son had so suddenly disappeared, and whose wife had died only a year before, was in his sixtieth year, and the additional shock of his only child, who was the sole heir to the wealthy Wilson estate, almost crazed him. I had known him for many years, and to him my father owed his start in his business career.

At the time of young Wilson's disappearance I was eighteen years of age. I had often read of the adventures and exploits of daring men who had stolen the children of wealthy people and retained them to reap a large reward.

I suggested to Mr. Wilson that such might be the fate of his son. The old gentleman, who was pondering over his great loss, suddenly gazed at me and said in an almost inaudible tone:

"Young man, I have thought of everything. I have believed that he was kidnapped; I have believed that he was drowned; then, again, that he was accidentally run over, yes, everything, but for God's sake, why have I not received some tidings from him!"

I hardly knew what reply to make, for Mr. Wilson's tone had fairly unnerved me. There before me sat a man who had everything that Art and Nature could supply, living in the most luxurious style, everything to gratify, and now suddenly as miserable as the poorest beggar of a London highway. I looked at the old gentleman and discovered that the tears were streaming down his furrowed cheeks I tried to enter a word of consolation, when he sprang to his feet, exclaiming with emotion!

"Young man, I will find that child if I have to spend my entire fortune. I have put the matter in the hands of my attorneys, Messers. Jennings & Compton, who have correspondents in every large city of the world. They have employed a corps of detectives, and have set to work in a most satisfactory manner, and assured me they will find my boy within a very short time."

When Mr. Wilson had finished I suggested that if

agreeable to him I would work upon the case myself, with the express stipulation that I should not be known in the matter, and should be retained without compensation. I had felt under obligations to the Wilsons, and would only be endeavoring to compensate them for their many kindnesses to my father, and, indeed to me.

"My dear boy," continued Mr. Wilson, "I would most gladly have you do anything you could to assist in finding my dear child, and so far as your not being compensated for your services, I shall not only give you the reward of $50,000, as advertised by Jennings & Compton, but shall give you $50,000 additional—anything to find my child."

"Well, Mr. Wilson," I continued, "I shall enter upon this work at once, and we shall not quarrel about any compensation, but I shall make this case my sole duty."

The old gentleman wiped his moistened eyes, and walked with me to his front door. As I was about to leave him he took from his pocket a small photograph which he gave me.

"This," he said, "may assist you somewhat in your efforts; guard it carefully."

I assured him I would do so.

"Let me know everything of your steps in this matter," continued Mr. Wilson, "and, if need be, employ any one you suggest to assist you."

"I will go home at once," I replied, "map out my course of action, and call on you to-morrow morning at ten o'clock. Until then, adieu."

So saying, the old gentleman shook my hand and embraced me, and cried as if his heart would break.

CHAPTER II.

TO those of my readers who have passed through a severe nervous excitement I need not attempt to explain my feeling as I strode along towards my home; but to those who have always had the happiness of pursuing the even tenor of their way, unmolested by the many vicissitudes of life and not encountering ever and anon some terrible calamity, sickness and death itself, I wish to address a few remarks before drifting further. It had always been my fortune to possess an abundance of life's goods. Educated in the highest schools of London and graduating at Paris, I returned to my native city and entered into business with my father, with whom I soon became associated as junior partner. Our factories were supplying the Old and New Worlds with all kinds of silken goods and we employed several hundreds of hands, including clerks, etc. I was really manager of the entire business. Mr. Wilson's unbounded kindness towards my father and myself, and my desire to, in some manner, show my gratitude, had set me, as I promised him, to devise some plan for ascertaining the whereabouts of his lost son. And it did not take me long to do so. Knowing that the Fall trade would soon be opening and that our drummers would be leaving for the large cities, I conceived the idea of making each of them an assistant in my little detective scheme, instructing them in all details, and giving to each one a copy of the photograph of young Wilson, at the same time enjoining the strictest secrecy in their workings. I had told my father of my plan and made arrangements by which I should start for Paris.

Hardly had the morning dawned when I arose, partook of a slight breakfast, and directed my footsteps to Mr. Wilson's residence. As I knocked at the door, the old gentleman came out saying:

"Good morning; I have been watching for you."

"Why," I replied, "do you know it's but eight o'clock, and I promised to call at ten; but could not wait, I was so anxious to see you and tell you my plan."

"Ah, yes, but I did not have a moment's sleep last night and really did not know the hour; I can do nothing but think and think. For God's sake do something to restore my boy to me;" and the poor man sank back in his chair with a death-like pallor upon his face.

"Well, now, Mr. Wilson, we have a plan that will certainly do some good. I have instructed each one of our drummers to act as a sort of a detective. You know they start in a few days to work up the Fall trade and can be of wonderful assistance to us in looking for Tyler. You know my belief is that he is not in London. I really think he is in Paris, and I have arranged with Father so I can go to that city within a few days and intend to work there upon my plan, keeping you advised daily of my action."

"Well," interrupted Mr. Wilson, "you seem to talk most hopefully. God grant that your efforts will be successful, and I shall certainly die a happy man. The plan that you have suggested is certainly a novel one and will undoubtedly be of some service. Whatever you need to defray the expenses incident to it, please let mo pay. I most assuredly do not wish you to undertake this matter and spend money without being reimbursed, and——"

"Mr. Wilson," I interrupted, "I consider that whatever I can do for you is simply a return of gratitude. Father has often told me of your goodness and kindness towards him; for myself, I can never repay you for your generosity towards me. I shall, however, attempt to make some return, and intend devoting every moment of my time in assisting in the search for your son; and, now, with your sanction, I shall commence upon the plan I have suggested."

"My sanction!" exclaimed Mr. Wilson, "that you have without a doubt, and may God bless your steps."

It was now 10 o'clock, and as I had written to my confidential clerk to meet me at my house at 10:30 I took my departure, promising to return by the next morning.

CHAPTER III.

AS I was entering my house, I was accosted by a Frenchman, evidently about forty years of age. "Good morning," he commenced; have I the pleasure of addressing Mr. Park?"

"That is my name, sir," I replied.

"Well, I have a letter of introduction to you, from Mr. E. Cabel Slavin of Paris," continued the Frenchman, at the same time drawing a letter from his inner coat pocket.

I read the letter introducing Monsieur Andro Le Dreux, "a gentleman of high social and financial standing, starting on a pleasure trip, combined with business, in London."

Excusing myself for a moment, I went into my study.

"Well, I did not expect to be so long away," I remarked, addressing my confidential clerk. "I will see you in a few moments. There is a gentleman waiting for me in the parlor. He has just come from Paris, with a letter of introduction from my old friend, Slattery."

"Why is that fellow in there?" asked Mr. Pixley. (That was my clerk's name.)

"Yes, I told him to wait a few moments when I would return."

"Well, said Pixley, "he has been waiting here for about an hour, and I imagined you had employed him to write your biography. He asked me question after question—where you had your office, when you commenced business, your age, how many clerks you employed, your full name, your father's full name, and Heaven knows what not! Don't you know that man looks like Sellers who left London some ten or twelve years ago, between two days, and I really believe he wears a wig. You take particular notice of him and see if his eyebrows, moustache and hair are not all different in color. I was particularly impressed by his accent; it really seemed assumed."

"Well, Pixley, you have made a rather minute description of the Frenchman. I will go and see him and return in a few minutes."

Entering the parlor, Mr. Le Dreux arose and shook hands with me, remarking:

"Well, I feel that I have known you for years; it seems that I must have seen you in Paris."

"No," I replied, "I don't remember seeing you in Paris, though I annually visit that city."

Mr. Le Dreux had seated himself directly in front of a large mirror, and I had been thinking all the time of Pixley's remark of the wig and hair, and I had soon become convinced that Pixley was correct in his surmise. The Frenchman undoubtedly wore a wig. His eyebrows were very dark; his moustache lighter, while the hair was of an auburn hue.

"Well," I commenced, "you left Mr. Slattery in Paris?"

"Yes; I saw him the day I embarked. He informed me that he would probably be over to London in a week or two and would call on you."

"Mr. Park," continued the Frenchman, "I have come to see you upon a matter of great importance. You have no doubt heard of the sudden and mysterious disappearance of a young boy by the name of Tyler Edgar Wilson, of your city?"

"Yes," I replied, "I have heard of it, and have only this morning seen the poor father, who is nearly dead with grief at the loss of his child."

"Yes," continued Mr. Le Dreux, "it is a very sad thing. I was first informed of it through the newspapers, where I noticed the article by the attorneys having charge of the case. I presume the lad has been kidnapped by some parties knowing the immense wealth of his father, and are endeavoring to get a big reward."

"Well," I suggested, "don't you think a reward of fifty thousand dollars is sufficient?"

The Frenchman gave a little hectic cough, as though he was trying to save time in which to gather thoughts for reply.

"Oh, yes—why—well," he finally stammered; "I should have said that some one who does not know of the large reward offered is retaining the boy."

"I don't know, indeed; but it seems to me anyone holding him for that purpose would certainly watch the newspapers; and then, again, notices of the reward have been conspicuously displayed throughout London."

As I finished talking I noticed that Mr. Le Drenx had taken the small charm dangling from his watchchain and held it fixedly towards me, not noticing that I was at the time observing him.

"Do you know," he commenced, "I should like very much to meet Mr. Wilson, the unfortunate father of the missing boy? I have somehow had a desire to assist in working on this case."

"Indeed," I said; "and have you come to London for that purpose?"

"Well, not exactly; but I thought that I might be of some service in the matter, and not knowing any one in London, requested my friend, Mr. Slattery, to give me a letter of introduction to a friend of his. He suggested that he knew you very well and that your acquaintance with London would be of great assistance to me."

Here was a most novel thing. A man whom I had never seen before, from the French Capital, and visiting me to interest himself in the search of a young boy, who, like myself, he did not know. Pausing for a moment (for I really had to reflect upon the strange occurrence before me) I looked into the eyes of the man.

"Mr. Le Dreux, do you know anything about this case—have you ever seen young Tyler Wilson?" I asked.

"Certainly not. I have not the slightest acquaintance with the Wilsons—never knew them. I have become interested in the young boy through sympathy for his poor parents, for I am sure they are heartbroken."

"Well," I continued, "I should like very much to have you see Mr. Wilson, and if you will call this afternoon, we will go together, at four o'clock."

"Perfectly satisfactory," replied Mr. Le Dreux, and he bowed himself out promising to be prompt in keeping his engagement.

CHAPTER IV.

UPON entering my study, I discovered that Pixley had gone to sleep on the sofa. Arousing him, he opened his eyes in an enquiring manner, at the same time suggesting that he had better apologize for taking a nap during business hours.

"That is all right," I consoled him. "You, no doubt, were made tired by that Frenchman, and I feel myself like dozing even as I stand here."

"By the way"—and Pixley started up—"don't they want me at the office to-day?"

"No; I wish you, to-day, right here. I have something that is very urgent and will require your services for the rest of this afternoon. But, before we proceed further, I wish you would go into the parlor and get me that Frenchman's card; I want to get his full name."

Pixley returned with the small visiting card and at the same time was reading a scrap of paper.

"Pixley, what are you trying to decipher?" I asked.

"Well, I don't know what it is, but you can probably distinguish the letters better than I.".

"Why, it is very legible, it is Tellers—A. S. Tellers," I answered.

"Great Heavens!" exclaimed Pixley, "where did you get that paper?"

"Why, you just gave it to me. Didn't you bring it in with that Frenchman's card? What is the reason you are so startled?"

Pixley took the slip of paper and read it again, and then exclaimed:

"That name is A. S. Sellers. You remember, I told you that I thought that Frenchman resembled Sellers, who left London some years ago? Now, there is something very mysterious about that man, Le Dreux. Did you notice his hair?"

"Yes; I certainly did."

"And his accent? Don't you think it is assumed?"

"Well, I don't know; it was rather peculiar," I replied.

"Mr. Park, have you any objection to your telling

me what Mr. Le Dreux called for? I am certainly interested in this matter, and I am almost certain that he is the same Sellers of whom I spoke;" and Pixley's face took on a glow of excitement.

"Well, Pixley, to answer your question brings us to the point, for which I summoned you here. Of course, you know about the great loss Mr. Wilson has just sustained; you know that it is to him Father owes his success in business, and, consequently, I also am indebted to him. I have promised to enlist in the duty of finding young Tyler, and for that purpose will leave for Paris within a few days. There is something prompting me that the boy is not in London. I feel confident he has been stolen by some one who is trying to reap a harvest, and it will be my aim to restore the boy to his father, and, if possible, without one cent of reward to any one. I remember reading in a paper a few years ago of an organized body of men in Paris who were engaged in the nefarious business of kidnapping the children of rich parents and withholding them for large sums of money. I shall make every effort to ascertain the abodes of these men, and through the assistance of the Police Department think I shall encounter but little difficulty. The Frenchman, Mr. Le Droux, has also volunteered his services, and he has promised to return this afternoon at four for the purpose of calling with me to meet Mr. Wilson."

Pixley grew amazed, and sarcastically remarked that "'A friend in need is a friend indeed.' I certainly cannot understand that Frenchman or his mission. You say you never saw him before?"

"Well, Pixley," I replied, "there is the letter of introduction he brought me."

Pixley's face was a study. He could not fathom that Frenchman, and, I must confess, he was an enigma to me, also.

"I have devised a scheme of my own, Pixley, that I am going to follow with reference to the search for young Tyler, and think success will attend my efforts. I have instructed all the drummers to act in the capacity of detectives while away, and to report to me daily as to any information obtained. In this manner I shall have quite a corps engaged in this work. All my letters are to be opened by you, and you shall forward them to me to the address I will give. Father is acquainted with my intention and has agreed to my leaving for Paris. I wish you to keep my address in Paris a secret, for I shall travel *incognito* while there. I shall have all my letters forwarded to the General Post Office and call for them.

"Now, you have the particulars with which I wished you to be acquainted, and as I have an appointment with Mr. Le Dreux, I shall not detain you longer, and——"

"But," interrupted Pixley, "let me ask you about Mr. Le Dreux. He is before me every moment; he seems so mysterious."

"Pixley," I replied, "I don't know anything about Le Dreux. I have not had much of an opportunity to judge of him. He is somewhat eccentric, I must confess. Why, don't you know when he was talking to me, he suddenly held his watch charm in front of me; I could not imagine what he was doing."

"Did you observe the charm particularly," inquired Pixley?

"Yes. It was a circular ornament, of the appearance of gold, and had a small hole in the centre."

"Well, I of course cannot be certain, Mr. Park," continued Pixley, "but I really believe from your description that the Frenchman's watch charm is a small detective kodak. I have seen them here in the city recently, and have read of them. I would certainly like to see the one Le Dreux has; what time will he be back?"

"Four o'clock."

"Well, I shall go to lunch and return so as to get another look at the Frenchman, and if possible his watch charm," and Pixley rose to go.

"You need not trouble yourself to go out to lunch for we shall go together—it is now ready," and Pixley and I entered the dining-room, where we did justice to our mid-day repast, and continued our conjectures as to the Frenchman.

CHAPTER V.

ENTERING my study I took up the morning paper, while Pixley busied himself with some memoranda pertaining to his duties as confidential clerk.

"Pardon me for interrupting you, Mr. Park, but I have just been studying over an idea that I conceived with reference to the search for young Tyler Wilson. I hope I do no injustice when I say that my impression as to Le Dreux is not altogether favorable. I have determined to watch that man, and if you have no objections, would like you to introduce me when he comes here this afternoon. Of course, he has met me, but I would like a formal introduction."

"Very well; whatever you suggest I will carry out, and I shall be glad to introduce you this evening to Le Dreux, and you can follow whatever plan you may wish to adopt. While personally I would not accept one pound of the reward Mr. Wilson has offered, I would be delighted to see the boy found, even if it were neceessary to pay every cent of the five thousand dollars out of my own pocket. However, if my supposition is correct, very little money will be required to obtain a clue. But what is your idea, Pixley? I should like to take counsel and receive suggestions before leaving for Paris."

"Well," began Pixley, "I have never had any practical experience as a detective, but must say that I have a theory of my own conception for working on a case like the one in question. You will no doubt agree with me that the manner of the Frenchman was most remarkable; and, when you stop to consider the facts, it seems a most astonishing coincident that a man bearing such a striking resemblance to Sellers—one of the most notorious rascals in London—should appear almost simultaneous with the loss of young Tyler Wilson. Sellers is liable to arrest whenever discovered here, and, if I mistake not, heavy reward for his conviction was advertised by the government. It is my intention to look for a clue in the direction of that very man Le Dreux."

"What! I exclaimed, "do you mean to say that you suspect him of being connected with the loss of the boy?"

"I have not said that, Mr. Park, but in the light of the most remarkable occurrence you have spoken of, and the impression Le Dreux has left upon my mind, I most certainly am of the opinion he can throw some light upon the whereabouts of Tyler Wilson."

"Well, do you suggest that I postpone my visit to Paris?" I inquired.

"Suppose you wait for a week and we will work together upon the case in London. My own opinion is that the boy will be found here in this very city."

"Pixley, you seem to have a strong repugnance for that man from Paris, and while I have believed that Tyler had disappeared from London, I will do as you suggest, and remain here a week longer and co-operate with you."

As I finished talking a servant entered and announced that a gentleman wished to see me. Going into the hall leading to the front door stood a man who addressed me at once as "Mr. Park."

"Excuse me," I replied, "but you have the advantage of me."

"Why, you know we met in Paris last Fall. My name is Renzé—Paul Renzé."

"Certainly, certainly," I replied. "I remember you now very well—won't you come into my study?"

"No, no; I have but a moment; I have just left my friend, Mr. Le Dreux, very ill at his hotel. It was by accident I learned of his visit to London and called to see him this afternoon, but only to find him confined to his bed, suffering from a severe attack of vertigo. He informed me of an appointment he had with you and requested me to call by and make his apology."

"Why, no apology is needed. I only regret that Mr. Le Dreux is unwell," I replied. "It must be most sudden, for he was apparently well when he called on me yesterday."

"Yes; but he tells me he is subject to such attacks."

"Do you intend returning to the hotel immediately to see Mr. Le Dreux?" I inquired.

"Yes; I promised him to be back within the next hour. He wishes me to send some dispatches to his family."

"Well, I suppose I shall have the pleasure of a call from you soon;" I suggested.

"It would, I assure you Mr. Park, afford me much delight to call upon you again before returning to Paris, but I have made arrangements for leaving by tomorrow evening. However, I shall be back within the next month, as I have some important matters before the courts, and shall without fail visit you."

"Pardon me, but did Mr. Le Dreux say anything to you about Mr. Wilson?"

"Mr. Wilson? No, I am not acquainted with that gentleman," replied Renzé.

"Well, Mr. Le Dreux and I had made an appointment to call this afternoon to see Mr. Wilson. You know his son suddenly disappeared from London a short time ago, and it has been impossible to obtain any knowledge of his whereabouts. His father has offered a reward of fifty thousand dollars for his return."

"Indeed, such things were common in Paris some years ago, but the police and a secret society of that city finally succeeded in eradicating the organization engaged in the scheme of stealing children, and," continued Mr. Renzé, "my friend, Mr. Le Dreux, was one of the prime movers in destroying this band of diabolical schemers."

"Is that a fact?" I inquired in astonishment. "Mr. Le Dreux has kindly offered to assist in the search for young Tyler Wilson, and it was with reference to this he intended to call this evening."

"Well, if you can secure his services you will be fortunate. He is not only a man of great influence, but also very wealthy, and can no doubt render great aid in this case;" and Mr. Renzé took his watch, and observing the hour, turned to leave, suggesting that it was not his intention of remaining so long from his friend, Mr. Le Dreux.

"Excuse me, but if you can wait but a moment, I should like you to meet a friend of mine who is in my study;" and I called to Pixley, and introduced him.

We talked together and for several minutes, when Mr. Ronzé took his departure promising to return again within a month's time.

CHAPTER VI.

IT was now three o'clock, and I must confess I felt a growing interest in my plan as suggested to Pixley; that my interest in Mr. Le Dreux was aroused to the highest pitch, was quite apparent; and it was with difficulty I refrained from calling upon Mr. Wilson to inform him of my new acquaintance, and the hope of getting another follower in the increasing list of volunteers anxious to assist in restoring to Mr. Wilson his darling child. However, I concluded to wait until the following day, intending to call to see Mr. Le Dreux, and go with him to Mr. Wilson.

Pixley had returned to the study-room, where I joined him.

"Well, have you been conceiving any new plans?" I asked.

"No, I have but one; that I shall work for the present."

"I am sorry that you did not have an opportunity of seeing Le Dreux this evening. His illness is very sudden. His friend, Mr. Renzé, informed me it was an attack of vertigo, to which he was subject."

"By the way, I intended asking you about Le Deux's friend," said Pixley. "You stated that he was from Paris. Do you know him personally?"

"Well, I was introduced to him some time ago while in Paris. I met him one evening at the hotel where I was stopping. We soon became quite intimate, and entered with two other gentlemen into a game of cards. It was simply a little social game. The stakes were not large at any time, and I did not realize it when I arose that I was a loser to the extent of five hundred dollars. Renzé, and the gentleman to whom he introduced me, but whose name I cannot recall, were partners. It was the only game I played with these gentlemen while in Paris, for I soon learned that they were adepts at the game and frequently visited Monte Carlo. However, we saw each other very often, and in that way became rather well acquainted. Renzé, in particular, was a very pleasant gentleman, and we spent many an hour together in the evening when I returned to the hotel."

"Did you notice the small emblem Mr. Renzé had in the lapel of his coat?" inquired Pixley.

"Yes, I did; that, I think, is a masonic emblem, and I think Le Dreux has one similar."

"I think you are correct; it is a masonic emblem. I would like to know the significance of the letters 'S. S. T.' I presume they are the initials of some password;" and Pixley drew from his coat a small book, in which he proceeded to write.

"What are you doing now," I inquired; "another inspiration?"

"No; I am simply noting in this book, which is but a diary, everything that occurs in connection with my little detective scheme; it may be of use in the future. Now, for instance, I will enter under this date that I met Mr. Paul Renzé, a friend of Mr. Le Dreux, giving at the same time a description of his appearance, etc."

"A very clever idea, Pixley. It did not occur to me to keep a book as you have done, but I shall do so, and with your permission will copy what you have already noted. I presume you have been entering everything you consider of importance from the beginning?"

"Certainly; from the very moment you spoke to me of the matter, I have entered in this little book every scrap of information bearing upon the subject. I was particular to make a minute entry of everything you told me of Le Dreux, because to him I shall turn my attention. He, I know, can give me some points, or I am greatly mistaken;" and Pixley smiled as he handed me his book.

"Thanks; I will copy from this and give it to you in the morning, Pixley," I said. "Can you not stay for dinner, and we will go to the Post-office together, for I expect an important letter."

"Well, if you wish me to accompany you to the

Postoffice, I will do so," said Pixley; " but I must beg to be excused from remaining for dinner, as I have a few personal matters to look after before night. I will go home and return in about an' hour."

So saying, Pixley arose and departed.

CHAPTER VII.

RINGING for my servant he informed me that dinner would be ready in about twenty minutes. "All right," I replied, "call me; I will remain in my study."

I began to ponder over Pixley's novel idea as to keeping a full account of all that transpired in reference to the loss of poor Tyler Wilson. Taking out the small note book, I commenced to copy into a book which I discovered in my desk. As I proceeded the manner of Pixley's "notes" became more and more interesting. But now I had to pause—Pixley had been attempting some drawing or was evidently endeavoring to delineate something; just what, I could not decipher. Finally, after much thought, I remembered the masonic emblem that Mr. Renzé wore. It was this that Pixley had drawn in his book.

"Well," I said to myself, "Pixley is certainly exact in his descriptions. He undoubtedly is interested in his new work; and will very likely give some valuable assistance to me."

At this point dinner was announced, and calling my servant I requested him to summons a messenger. In the meantime I wrote the following letter to Mr. Wilson:

My Dear Mr. Wilson: Tuesday.

   I regret exceedingly my inability to see you to-day. I had intended calling, but have been prevented by several reasons. I will see you to-morrow without fail. In the meantime I would suggest that you refer every one inquiring as to the loss of Tyler to your attorneys. My motive for this suggestion I will explain when I see you.
          Sincerely yours,   T. Lenox Park.

Handing the letter to the messenger I entered the dining-room, but was unable to eat. My appetite had entirely disappeared, though but a short time before I was extremely hungry. I was at a loss to account for this, but consoled myself that I was feeding upon an interesting subject, which I confess was ever before me, and which not only prevented my eating, but also was the cause of sleepless nights. Taking a cup of strong coffee, I arose and returned to my study and resumed the copying of Pixley's notes. Hardly had I finished when the servant informed me that Pixley himself was awaiting me in the parlor. As I entered Pixley handed me the evening paper, calling my attention to an article stating that a young man had been discovered alongside of the railroad on the outskirts of London. From his position he had evidently been thrown or fallen under the wheels of a passing train. There was nothing by which he could be identified, but his description corresponded almost exactly to that of young Wilson.

"My Heavens!" I exclaimed, as I finished reading, "it certainly cannot be Tyler; but who knows. I hope Mr. Wilson has not seen that article. Bad news always travels fast, and some one will undoubtedly tell him of this article in the paper. I have just sent him a note by courier telling him I would see him to-morrow, and in the meantime to refer all inquiries as to Tylor to his lawyers."

"What was your intention in doing that?" asked Pixley.

"Well, I will tell you. Your remarks about that man, Le Dreux, have made me very suspicious about him. It occurred to me that he might know something of Tyler's whereabouts, and might also call on Mr. Wilson to obtain some information from him."

"Yes, I see," said Pixley. "You are gradually being converted to the belief that I had from the first moment I learned of the cause of Le Dreux's visit here—that is, that he is able to enlighten you considerably in searching for Mr. Wilson's son."

"But what makes you so positive in your assertion, Pixley?"

"Simply my belief that Le Dreux is no more or less than A. S. Sellers, himself; Le Dreux is in disguise."

"Oh, I see you mean that Le Dreux is French for Sellers," and Pixley laughed at my little joke."

"Well, if you are ready, Pixley, we will start for the Post-office."

"Then we will be going," and Pixley and I hastened to catch a passing car, but only to be too late.

"So much the better," said I, "it will give us a much better opportunity to talk without being heard; and, as I told you, everything must be kept most secret."

CHAPTER VIII.

THE night was perfect. The stars were sparkling like clustered diamonds. The Milky Way was discernible in all its beauty, and the entire dome of Heaven was resplendent in the fullness of its glory. Hither and thither the bustling crowd was ever passing.

"Pixley, did you ever pause for a moment to reflect upon the multitude that throngs our city? Did you ever stop to consider how they eko out an existence?"

"What is the matter; your thoughts are drifting to various shores;" and Pixley gave a hearty smile. "But to answer your question. Yes, I have often thought of the mass of humanity surging through our city day after day, and likewise reflected and conjectured as to their manner of living. One man lives in elegance and opulence, while another dies in squalor and without the very necessaries of life. Often and often have I wished that it were within my power to rectify the existing inequalities of our day. But what would my frail efforts avail." And Pixley gave a heavy sigh.

"Yes, it is unfortunate," I said, "that such should be the condition of affairs. The poor are driven to all kinds of vice and have to resort to dishonorable means for their maintenance. But," I continued, "it is not only the poorer classes who are addicted to culpable acts, but the rich, also. They are not satisfied with what should be considered sufficient, but their avaricious nature and passion for accumulation blind them to the rights of their fellow-men, of whom they take every advantage."

"Alas! too true; and to the rich more than the poor is attributable the inequalities of our times; and to some rich rascal may be traced the loss of young Tyler Wilson."

"What!" I asked, surprised at Pixley's remark. "Did you not say only a few hours ago that you suspected Le Dreux—or, rather that, to use your own words, 'he could throw some light upon the matter'?"

"Exactly so. I said that it was my opinion that to some rich rascal might be traced Tyler's loss. And did Le Dreux's letter of introduction not say he was a man of high social and financial standing? That was my recollection."

"Ah! I see; you have simply another *nom de plume* for the Frenchman;" and Pixley laughed heartily at my remark.

Noticing the hour, we quickened our pace and arrived at the Post-office. Getting my mail, I hailed a cab, and Pixley and I drove home together.

"Won't you come in, Pixley?" I asked.

"No, it is rather late, but I will call around early in the morning; good-night," and Pixley started for his home.

I went to my study and began opening my mail. They nearly all pertained to orders for our silken goods. Taking one of the envelopes in my hand, I was at once interested in the peculiar style of writing. Well, evidently the writer does not know me very well, for he has my name spelled incorrectly. I wonder from whom it can be. Finally I opened the envelope and was surprised to find the letter dated " London."

"Well," I remarked to myself as I finished reading; " here is a conundrum. Some one has evidently learned of my interest in Mr. Wilson and my desire to assist in the search for his child. I wonder if it can be a hoax?" And I again took up the letter and read and reread. It was as follows:

DEAR SIR: LONDON.
If Mr. Wilson desires to see his son again he had better increase the reward he has advertised. Fifty thousand dollars is a trifle for him to pay. You can reach me through the " Personal Column " of the " *Evening* ——," where I will look for your answer. If Mr. Wilson is wise he will not delay. FENNILÉ.

Putting the letter in my pocket I hastened to my bedroom. It was impossible to sleep. Everything imaginable was passing through my mind. Now Le Dreux would be before me, and I would study and study over the possibility of his being a deceitful rascal, as Pixley was wont to believe. Hardly had I vanished these thoughts when my newly-received letter would flash before me in all its realism, so distinct that I could read the words and see the mysterious signature of "Fennilé." And so the night passed without a moment's rest, and I gladly welcomed the approach of daylight.

CHAPTER IX.

HAVING finished breakfast, I entered my study and began reading the morning paper. Quickly scanning the different items of interest, I went out the front door, where I met Pixley.

"Good morning, Pixley. I am glad you have come. I've a new chapter for your note-book; just come in."

I handed Pixley the latest news—the letter from "Fennilé."

"What do you think of that, Pixley?"

"Well, I don't really know what to say." And Pixley was astonishment itself. He took the letter, read it again, examined it carefully, and handed it to me, at the same time inquiring:

"When did you receive that interesting letter?"

"Last night, when we went to the Post-office."

"Do you think it possible to obtain any information as to "Fennilé" by calling at the office of the *Evening* ——? If you approve, we might go by the office this morning and make some inquiry."

"No, Pixley, I don't think it well to appear too hasty. I am going to see Mr. Wilson this morning and will show him the 'Fennilé' letter."

"There's some one ringing," remarked Pixley.

"Yes; the servant is at the door," and at that moment I heard Mr. Le Dreux's voice.

I did not wait for my servant to bring me his card, but entered the parlor.

"Why I am glad to see you out again. Sorry you were unwell yesterday."

"Oh, a little attack of dizziness. I'm all right, now. I was extremely sorry we could not see poor Mr. Wilson. Have you heard from him?"

"No," I replied, "but if you are well enough we will call on him this morning."

"Very nice, very nice," and Mr. Le Dreux rose to get his hat.

"Excuse me one moment, Mr. Le Dreux," and I went into the study for Pixley.

"Pixley," I said, "your friend, the Frenchman, is in the parlor; now is your opportunity to get an introduction and make some 'notes.'"

Pixley smiled, remarking that the Frenchman was a friend inasmuch as he belongs to the general brotherhood of man. Pixley expressed his delight at being introduced and was most attentive to every word he uttered. Now he was studying his face, the hair, observing the poor Frenchman at every turn.

"Well," I suggested, " if you are ready, Mr. Le Dreux, we will start for Mr. Wilson's."

Mr. Le Dreux quickly acquiesced, and we walked out into the beautiful morning air, discoursing as to the probable chances of our finding Mr. Wilson at home. We had not gone far before Pixley became very talkative with Mr. Le Dreux, and I smiled within myself as I thought of his great suspicion of the Frenchman, who apparently was very much interested in Pixley's loquacious manner.

"I perceive," remarked Pixley, "that you are a member of some masonic society."

"Oh, no. You allude to my emblem?"

"Yes; I thought it was a masonic insignia."

"No, it is the emblem of a society in Paris, of which I have honor of being a member. How long will it take us to reach Mr. Wilson's?" inquired Le Dreux abruptly changing the subject.

"We will be there in about half an hour," I replied.

"My reason in making the inquiry is, I wish to be back to my hotel and answer some correspondence in time for the evening post."

"You shall have ample time," I replied; "I have work of the same nature to perform."

"I was pleased to see our mutual friend, Mr. Renzé, last evening," I remarked to Mr. Le Dreux.

"Yes, he is a very clever fellow. It was too bad he has to return to Paris so soon, but he will be back, he tells me, within a month."

"You knew Mr. Renzé in Paris?" I asked Le Dreux.

"Oh, certainly. Very well. We have been acquainted many, many years."

"I had the pleasure of meeting Mr. Renzé, in Paris, and we had many pleasant hours together while I stopped at the hotel. He is quite a good card player, I believe?"

Mr. Le Dreux's face changed, I noticed, at my remark as to Renzé's proficiency at cards, and in an animated voice replied:

"Well, I have never played a game of cards in my life; as for Mr. Renzé, I have not heard of his playing. What elegant building is that?" inquired Mr. Le Dreux, again adroitly changing the conversation.

"Why, that is Mr. Wilson's residence," I replied.

"Yes, and it is the oldest mansion in this section of London," said Pixley.

"It is certainly a grand dwelling, a fit castle for a wealthy gentleman," remarked Mr. Le Dreux.

"There is Mr. Wilson, now;" and Pixley pointed out the old gentleman sitting on his front piazza.

"Poor man!" I exclaimed; "he is almost heartbroken."

"Yes, it is sad," ejaculated Mr. Le Dreux. "I only hope we can devise some means for restoring his lost son."

Reaching the house we were met by a servant, who announced our arrival and we were met in a few moments by Mr. Wilson, who walked with feeble step and who was fast showing the effects of the terrible loss he had recently sustained.

I introduced Mr. Le Dreux, who informed Mr. Wilson of his mission. The old gentleman listened earnestly and said with a sigh, as Mr. Le Dreux concluded:

"My good friend, accept my sincere thanks for your sympathy. It is somewhat consoling to know that I have so many kind friends who are so willing to assist in the search for my dear boy. I would give my entire fortune to see him once again."

The poor man was overcome. He buried his face in his hands and sobbed bitterly.

It was with difficulty that I restrained my emotions; when I saw Mr. Wilson weeping I felt that I would willingly sacrifice my life to restore to him his lost child.

"Mr. Wilson, I received a very mysterious communication last night. It was among my letters;" and I drew from my pocket the letter received from "Fennilé."

Mr. Wilson took the letter and read it several times. Returning it to me, he said:

"I wonder why it was sent to you; certainly every one knows that Jennings & Compton have charge of the case. I certainly think that it was written by a crazy person. What can they want, if they are not satisfied with the reward I offered?"

"Well," I replied, "you know as much about it as I, Mr. Wilson. The letter was received by me last evening and I have shown it to no one but yourself and Mr. Pixley."

"Pardon me, but may I look at that letter," said Mr. Le Dreux, at the same time extending his hand.

"Certainly," handing it to him, remarking that it was perhaps a hoax, or, as Mr. Wilson suggested, the work of a crazy person.

"Oh, I hardly think any one could be so cruel as to play a trick of that kind," said Mr. Le Dreux. "My own opinion is that 'Fennilé' either knows the whereabouts of the boy or perhaps wants to be retained in the case."

Returning the letter to my pocket, I suggested that we better be leaving, for I had some other matters of importance to be attended to before evening.

Mr. Wilson escorted us to the door, and as I reached for my hat he said: "Excuse me a moment, but I would like to see you, Mr. Park," and I returned with him to the piazza.

"I received your note last evening, requesting me to say nothing about Tyler's loss until you saw me. You said you would explain your reason for this suggestion when you saw me."

"Yes, Mr. Wilson; I did not like to say anything about it in the presence of Mr. Le Dreux. Pixley is rather suspicious of him, and, I must confess, has made me also a little anxious to ascertain something about that Frenchman. He called upon me a few days ago with a letter of introduction from a friend of mine in Paris, Mr. Slattery, who stated that Le Dreux was of high standing, financially and otherwise, and was to visit London for business, combined with pleasure. This is all I know of him. He informed me he had heard of your loss through the papers and was at once seized with the desire to assist you. I told him I knew you very well, and if he so desired, would introduce him to you. Hence our visit. Pixley has a little scheme of his own conception. He tells me he expects to have light thrown upon the whereabouts of Tyler in the direction of Le Dreux himself; and as Pixley has requested me to postpone my visit to Paris, I will co-operate with him in searching for information here."

"Why! Do you think that Mr. Le Dreux is playing the part of a hypocrite?" asked Mr. Wilson.

"Well, I don't like to do any one an injustice, but Pixley has formed a most unfavorable opinion as to the Frenchman, and says he is going to work on him for some valuable points."

"Then, do you think I had better request him to

withdraw his proffered services for the present?" ask[ed]
Mr. Wilson.

"No; I would not do that now. Give him a chan[ce]
and we will soon find him out. I will keep you a[d]-
vised of everything. But I would suggest that y[ou]
direct him to confer hereafter either with your att[or]-
neys or me. As long as he has expressed a willingness [to]
assist without compensation, we are able to retain hi[m]
without loss.

"Then, I shall do as you suggest," said Mr. Wils[on.]

We walked together to the door, where I apologiz[ed]
for detaining Mr. Le Dreux and Mr. Pixley, and bi[d]-
ding "good-bye" to Mr. Wilson, we departed.

CHAPTER X.

"WE were detained longer than we anticipated, I remarked," seeing that there was a dearth of conversation.

"But we have plenty of time," remarked Pixley. "If you simply wish to catch the evening post, there are two hours remaining to you."

Mr. Le Dreux, I noticed, seemed rather indifferent as to our conversation.

"You seem wrapped in thought, Mr. Le Dreux," I remarked.

"Yes, I was thinking of the great affliction that sometimes befalls us when we seem in the enjoyment of everything. As I looked around me in Mr. Wilson's mansion, I could not refrain feeling that his loss, indeed, was a sad one, and I have been thinking of what I could do to assist in the search for the missing boy."

"Well, I would be glad to have you co-operate with me, Mr. Le Dreux, if you have no objection. I have a plan of my own and have already enlisted a number of my friends, and have no doubt we shall accomplish something.

"Indeed, I should be pleased to hear your plan, and should also like to give whatever aid I can, but I should consider it a good idea to have this matter put in the hands of some good detectives."

As Mr. Le Dreux concluded his remarks, he took from his pocket a small card, which he handed to me.

"Those gentlemen," he said, "are the best detectives in Paris. They were formerly employed by the Government, but are now engaged in business for themselves. I would suggest that it may be wise to communicate with them and get their co-operation, also."

"It may be that they are already engaged on this case," I remarked. "Messrs. Jennings & Compton, the attorneys employed by Mr. Wilson, have correspondents in all the large cities, and have, no doubt, engaged the services of some one in Paris."

"Well, if Mr. Wilson would not object, I would like to write to Messrs. Jennot & Straitton, for I have confidence in their ability."

"You might see him, and see what he thinks of your suggestion."

"Then I shall call upon him to-morrow, for I am anxious to do as much as possible before returning to Paris."

"Do you intend returning shortly?" I inquired.

"In about a week or ten days," replied Mr. Le Dreux.

"Oh, I had expected you would remain longer."

"It was my intention of doing so, but I last evening received a letter announcing the loss of some property I owned, and I am obliged to be present in the adjustment of the insurance."

"That is bad news, but I hope your property was fully insured," I remarked.

"I don't know the exact loss, but expect to receive the particulars within a day or two."

"Do you intend returning to London, Mr. Le Dreux?" I asked.

"Certainly; as soon as I have the matter of insurance settled."

"Then we shall see more of you, and can work much better than by corresponding."

We had now reached my home, and Pixley suggesting that I had some letters to get off by the next mail, Mr. Le Dreux bade us "good-bye," promising to call again the next day.

CHAPTER XI.

"WELL, Pixley, we had better be writing those letters, and I will dictate them to you now." I soon finished as the letters nearly all were very short, being simply letters of advice to our foreign correspondents, and related to the purchase of goods for the fall trade. The most important letter, as it afterwards proved to be, was one I sent to Messrs. Jennings & Compton, enclosing the communication I had received from "Fennilé." I wrote to those gentlemen telling them of the peculiar letter, and requested that they keep its contents a secret until I should see them, which would be within a day or two, when I would also give them certain other information which might be of interest. I had reference to my meeting Mr. Le Dreux, and Pixley's unfavorable opinion of him.

"Well, Pixley, what have you gathered to-day for your note-book?" I asked.

Pixley smiled.

"Why, I have valuable points to-day, very valuable. The more I see of that Frenchman the more he becomes a mystery to me. Did you notice the abrupt manner in which he turned the conversation when he was asked about that emblem he wore?"

"Yes," I answered.

"And about Renzé?"

"I certainly did, but did not give it any particular thought."

"Well, I did, and I also noticed that the letters on the emblem were the same as those on Renzé's—'S. S. T.'—I should certainly like to know their meaning.

My opinion is that the 'S. S.' stands for 'Secret Society.'"

"Pixley, you are a keen observer," I remarked. "I did not remember the inscription on Renzé's emblem."

"I am now going to enter my minutes of to-day's proceedings;" and Pixley took out his book and began writing.

"Well, you might as well tell me of your minutes, as you have termed them, that I may also enter them in my book."

"Very, well; I shall do so."

"First," began Pixley. "Frenchman secretive as to society emblem."

"Second.—Evidently averse to talking of Renzé's card playing."

"Third.—Asked to see letters from Fennilé."

"Fourth.—Suggested that Jennot & Straitton of Paris be asked to assist."

"Is that all, Pixley?" I asked.

"Yes; all that occurred worth noting."

"Well, I see you evidently attribute some motive to Le Dreux's asking to see the Fennilé letter—what is it?"

"Oh, no," replied Pixley. "I simply have entered it as having occurred. All of these things may be of use in the future. I shall note everything that transpires so that I shall be kept posted as to the past;" and Pixley laughed as he returned his book to his pocket.

"Le Dreux will be here in the morning, and I think it would be well for him to see Jennings & Compton, and intend going with him. Will you care to go along?"

"Certainly; and I would like to accompany you whenever you go with that Frenchman, as I wish to see him as much as possible." And Pixley's face was wreathed in smiles.

"Very well, Pixley," I replied, "your wishes shall be carried out."

"I am sorry Le Dreux leaves London so soon, but when he returns you can have an opportunity of studying him. In the meantime, you can devote your time in the manner you deem best."

"Why don't you write to your friend Slattery and ask him something about Le Dreux's antecedents— how long he has known him; his business, etc.?" asked Pixley.

"I had intended doing that, but thought inasmuch as I should visit Paris so soon it could be deferred till then. I think our time can well be employed for the next few days, and hope, with our combined efforts, we can gather some important points; but, I must confess, my opinion has not changed. I still think that it will be useless to look for Tyler in the direction of London."

"Then," said Pixley, "I suggest that you remain in London no longer, but visit Paris as soon as possible. I shall devote every moment to searching for a clue here, while you can carry out your own plan in Paris."

"I agree with you, Pixley, but do not waste too much time on Le Dreux. While you have a very unfavorable opinion of him, and have also roused my suspicions as to him, I don't think he will be of any service to you one way or the other."

"All right. We will wait and see;" remarked Pixley, dryly.

"I shall now endeavor to arrange matters so I can leave for Paris within the next three days, Pixley, and should I leave before Le Dreux, keep my whereabouts unknown to him."

"Certainly; and as soon as you learn anything of him from your friend Slattery, advise me."

"Most undoubtedly," I replied. "Especially if it is anything unfavorable of him."

And we both joined in a hearty laugh over the idea that the poor Frenchman, who was apparently so anxious to render such valuable assistance in search of Mr. Wilson's son, was the object of gravest suspicion.

"Well, I have but a few minutes left in which to catch the post, and will take the letters, calling at Jennings & Compton on my way."

"That's a good idea, Pixley. They will get the letter earlier in the morning than if mailed. I hope you will be here before ten to-morrow."

"At any time you appoint," said Pixley; "daybreak, if necessary."

"Well, not quite so early; but say half-past nine, as your friend from Paris may be here, and I know you would not have him detained."

Pixley smiled, and remarking that he would do anything rather than inconvenience "that Frenchman," bade me good-evening and hastened to catch the evening post.

CHAPTER XII.

AS I sat in my study after Pixley's departure I began to ponder over the probability of our being able to gather from Mr. Le Dreux any clue as to Tyler Wilson. I had come to think that while Pixley was justly suspicious of him—for his sudden appearance upon the scene seemed a strange coincidence, occurring at about the same time as Tyler's mysterious disappearance—nothing material or of value to our case would be obtained in the direction of the Frenchman. Le Dreux's face had always seemed to be indicative of great anxiety and trouble. His wrinkled forehead protruded over a pair of small black eyes which peered at one in a most inquiring manner—in fact, as though the owner had great suspicion of the person at whom he was looking.

"Well, I most sincerely hope poor Pixley will be rewarded for his great interest and vigilance," I remarked to myself; "and I shall see that he is." So saying, I arose and entered the dining-room, where supper was awaiting. As I had missed my midday meal, I was somewhat hungry, and partook plentifully of all before me.

Finishing my supper, I returned to my study, where I sat till eleven o'clock writing instructions for Pixley to follow during my absence, with reference to his position as confidential clerk, and also in his new capacity as detective.

Taking the "Fennilé" letter I made a copy of it, filing the original in my desk. The copy I intended for Jennings & Compton, whom I should see the next morning and introduce Mr. Le Dreux, as Mr. Wilson had requested.

Though I was extremely fatigued, it was impossible to sleep; in fact, such I could say had been the case ever since I became interested in the search for Tyler Wilson. When night arrived I was anxious for the return of morning, that I might be able to again start out with my valuable assistant, Pixley, in carrying through our respective schemes. My great interest in the case had not only affected my sleeping hours, but likewise troubled me while awake. I finally had to allow Father to take entire charge of our business, for I was absorbed in my new work, and every day seemed like a year, so anxious was I to leave for Paris, that I might carry out my plan as originally proposed. I had felt almost beyond a doubt that my efforts in that city would result in the finding of Tyler.

As the first rays of the approaching daylight

streamed through the window of my room I arose and hastily dressed. As it would be some hours before breakfast, I concluded to take a walk, and strolled out into the morning air. The streets were fast becoming busy with the thousands hurrying to the different factories, shops and mercantile houses. Before I was aware I had reached our own business house, where, to my great surprise, I found Pixley.

"Good morning, Pixley, what are you doing here?" I asked.

"I have come down to open up and see whether your father did not want me to do something for him before calling on you."

"You are certainly the early bird," I replied; "have you had your breakfast?"

"Certainly, I am not too early to miss that duty," replied Pixley, smiling.

"Well, I was going to suggest that you go back and take breakfast with me."

"Thank you, but I most certainly did not expect to meet you here," said Pixley.

"It is somewhat of a surprise to me, Pixley; I did not know I was so near the store. I simply intended taking a walk as an appetizer, and before I knew it drifted here, and shall have to be hurrying back as they will be keeping breakfast awaiting me. I presume you will be up soon."

"Yes, I shall go as soon as I see your father."

"Well, then, I shall go."

My walk had given me a sharp appetite and I indeed enjoyed my breakfast meal.

Taking the morning paper I sat down in the study to await Pixley, and I had not been reading long when the servant announced that a gentleman who had been to see me before was awaiting me in the parlor.

I was greatly surprised to find, instead of Pixley, that it was Mr. Le Dreux.

"Well, I am glad to see you; I had not expected

you so early, but so much the better as it will give us more time," I remarked.

"That was exactly my reason in coming so soon. I know that lawyers are usually very busy and thought they could give us more of their time by calling on them early."

"Well, Pixley will be here in a few minutes and we shall then start together."

"Excuse me, but is that gentleman, Mr. Pixley, engaged in business with you?" asked Mr. Le Dreux.

"Yes; he is my confidential clerk."

"I see; he is also, I believe, associated with you in the search for Mr. Wilson's son."

"Oh, yes; I acquaint him with all my business and have also interested him in looking for a clue to Tyler Wilson's whereabouts."

"There he is now. I think the door bell is ringing,"

I was correct. Pixley had arrived and hearing my voice came in.

We did not remain many minutes, but went to Jennings & Compton.

Introduced Mr. Le Dreux, who explained his desire to assist Mr. Wilson in the search for his lost son. When he had finished, Mr. Jennings, the senior member of the firm, said:

"Mr. Le Dreux, we shall only be too happy to have you aid us, but we have, I think, discovered the lost boy. We are now working on a clue, and from reports received this morning feel confident we shall be successful in the very near future."

"Oh, I am so glad—where can he be?" asked Le Dreux in an excited voice.

"For the present we do not care to say much about it, lest we should not be fortunate in the ultimate finding of the boy," said Mr. Jennings.

Le Dreux took from his pocket a small card which he handed to Mr. Jennings, saying:

"That is a firm in Paris who have had great success in cases similar to the one in which you are now engaged. If you do not object I would suggest that you correspond with them, and, if possible, secure their services."

Mr. Jennings returned the card to Le Dreux, remarking that he had engaged the services of one of the best detectives in Paris as soon as Tyler Wilson had disappeared, and he was now devoting his entire energies to the matter.

Mr. Jennings arose and went into his private office. Excusing myself to Mr. Le Dreux and Pixley I followed.

As I entered, Mr. Jennings beckoned to me to sit down with him.

"Do you know that Mr. Le Dreux very well?" asked Mr. Jennings.

I explained to him the circumstances of his visit, the letter of introduction, etc. When I had concluded Mr. Jennings remarked:

"We will let him co-operate with us. But I must say it does seem strange that a man unknown to all of the parties directly concerned should evince so much apparent interest in this matter. I presume, of course, he is working for the fifty thousand dollar reward."

"No," I replied, "he tells me not. My own opinion was that he had probably met with a similar loss himself at the time and was desirous of assisting Mr. Wilson simply through sympathy for the old gentleman, but Pixley's suspicions of him have somewhat changed my mind, and I really do not know what to think."

"We will give him the benefit of the doubt and hope he will prove all right," remarked Mr. Jennings.

As we returned, Mr. Le Dreux had taken his hat and walked to the door.

"You are ready to go, I presume," I said, addressing Mr. Le Dreux.

"Yes."

We started down the street, and had gone but a few blocks when Le Dreux remarked that he had an engagement, and as it was near the hour, he would be leaving us, and he bade us good-bye, saying he would see us within a day or so.

A few minutes after Le Dreux had withdrawn, Pixley said:

"That man is a rascal, or I am no judge of human nature."

"To whom do you refer?" I asked.

"Why, that man, Le Dreux."

"What has he done now?"

"Well, when you were in Mr. Jenning's private office he became very talkative. He asked me if I knew anything of the new clue. I told him I did not; or had I heard anything about it. He then said that he thought it was a kind of bluff."

"Well, I don't see anything wrong in that remark, Pixley."

"Perhaps, you don't; but to me it seems very strange."

"Another thing," said Pixley; "I am certain I saw Le Dreux take some papers off Mr. Jennings' desk. As I turned around he was putting his hand in his inside coat pocket and was standing immediately in front of the desk."

"Pixley," I said; "you watch that poor Frenchman like a hawk watches a hen."

"Yes, and I shall continue to do so."

"I am going to Paris to-morrow, and you then shall have a good opportunity to see him oftener," I said.

"What, so soon?" said Pixley surprisedly, "I had expected you to remain for some days."

"It was my intention to do so, but matters have all been arranged, and as I am firm in my belief that Tyler is to be found in Paris, I have decided to delay no longer.

"Well, this is rather unexpected. I will go up and assist you to get off."

"Thanks; I have a letter of instructions that I also want to give you."

"Then," said Pixley, "you have additional directions for me?"

"Yes, pertaining to your course in the Tyler search."

We had now arrived at my house and after giving Pixley his letter of instructions we entered some minutes as to our mutual friend, the Frenchman.

"What are you going to enter now, Pixley?" I asked.

"Well, Le Dreux's remarks as to the clue, and also his taking the paper from the desk."

"Are you sure he took it?" I asked.

"Yes."

"Then why don't you report it to Mr. Jennings?"

"Well, I shall wait and shall give him a chance; probably he will return it."

"Just as you say, Pixley."

Lunch hour having arrived, I invited Pixley to join me. He, however, had no desire to eat, remarking that he did not have time to spare.

"Well, if you can do so conveniently, I wish you would purchase my ticket," and giving Pixley the money he started for the railroad office.

Hardly had I finished my luncheon when Pixley returned with my ticket.

"Now we shall proceed to dispatch the letter received this morning, and then I can say that I leave with a clear conscience."

And Pixley and I entered the study, which was also

used as an office room. There were but two or three letters, and unimportant too, and very easily answered.

"Pixley," I said, "I trust that during my absence you will see that Father does not overwork himself. You know he is not so young, now, and cannot work as much as when he was in the prime of life."

"Most assuredly. It will be my greatest aim to assist him," said Pixley.

"Did Mr. Jennings give you the name of the detective in Paris engaged upon the Wilson case?" inquired Pixley.

"No. I was about to ask him when I changed my mind. I had a delicacy about doing it."

"Well, if you so desire, I can call at the office this evening and ascertain for you."

"Never mind," I replied. "But you can inquire and send it to me when you write. But be sure that Le Dreux does not find it out."

"I shall be very careful about that, you can rest assured," replied Pixley.

"I shall keep you advised of anything I learn, and I wish you to write me daily as to your progress."

Pixley agreed to do so, and arose saying that as there seemed nothing further for him to do to assist me, he would be going to the office.

"Pixley, I want you to remain to dinner. This is the last time we can dine together until my return, and we can have an opportunity to talk over matters at the dinner table."

"Very well, I will do so. It seems to me we can probably suggest some further step for ascertaining quickly just why Lo Dreux has taken such great interest in Mr. Wilson's loss."

"Now, Pixley, I have told you that I have been of the opinion from the very beginning that young Tyler will never be found in London. I will let you work on the case here, and I will devote myself to searching for a clue in Paris."

"There is the dinner bell, now. Come, for I am very hungry, Pixley."

"That is something unusual for you, is it not?" said Pixley, smiling.

"Very true. This matter has taken away my appetite almost entirely."

"Precisely the same way with me," remarked Pixley, "but I feel that I can do justice to my dinner this evening."

We finished our meal and went upon the veranda where we mingled with the night air the fragrant fumes of our Havanas. We were suddenly interrupted by a messenger bringing a letter which I at once recognized as being from Le Dreux. He informed me that he had received a telegram that evening calling him to Paris and he would start by the next train, but would return in a week or ten days.

"It is very strange," said Pixley, as I finished reading Le Dreux's letter, "that he could not come to see you before leaving."

"Yes, it would appear so, but he may have been unable to do so," I replied.

It was now 10:30, and as it was very dark Pixley suggested that he would be going, promising to see me off by the morning train.

www.ingramcontent.com/pod-product-compliance
Lightning Source LLC
Chambersburg PA
CBHW020308090426
42735CB00009B/1266